our
Read-Aloud
FAMILY
journal

! ! !!

100 Books

the _____ Family
Shared Together!

How to Use this Journal...

!

1. Read a book aloud!

2. Record your family's book adventure!

- Write about: what you liked, your favorite characters, your favorite scenes, things that surprised you, things you learned, etc. Draw pictures, use stickers, anything you want!
- Have fun with it!
- Ask everyone in the family to contribute a memory to the journal. Build a beautiful record of your family's journey through 100 books.

3. Repeat 99 more times!
(share your progress with friends, #100bookstogether)

Table of Contents:
Our 100 Read-Aloud Books!

1. _____
2. _____
3. _____
4. _____
5. _____
6. _____
7. _____
8. _____
9. _____
10. _____
11. _____
12. _____
13. _____
14. _____
15. _____
16. _____
17. _____
18. _____
19. _____
20. _____

21. _____

22. _____

23. _____

24. _____

25. _____

26. _____

27. _____

28. _____

29. _____

30. _____

31. _____

32. _____

33. _____

34. _____

35. _____

36. _____

37. _____

38. _____

39. _____

40. _____

41. _____

42. _____

43. _____

44. _____

45. _____

46. _____

47. _____

48. _____

49. _____

50. _____

51. _____

52. _____

53. _____

54. _____

55. _____

56. _____

57. _____

58. _____

59. _____

60. _____

61. _____

62. _____

63. _____

64. _____

65. _____

66. _____

67. _____

68. _____

69. _____

70. _____

71. _____

72. _____

73. _____

74. _____

75. _____

76. _____

77. _____

78. _____

79. _____

80. _____

81. _____

82. _____

83. _____

84. _____

85. _____

86. _____

87. _____

88. _____

89. _____

90. _____

91. _____

92. _____

93. _____

94. _____

95. _____

96. _____

97. _____

98. _____

99. _____

100! _____

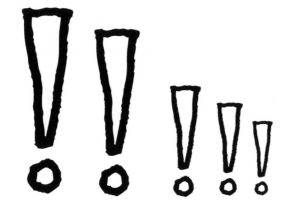

BOOK # _____   DATE: _____

Title: _____

Author: _____

Our Book Memories:

BOOK # _____   DATE: _____

Title: _____

Author: _____

Our Book Memories:

....

....

....

....

....

....

....

....

....

....

....

....

....

....

....

....

....

BOOK # _____   DATE: _____

Title: _____

Author: _____

Our Book Memories:

....

....

....

....

....

....

....

....

....

....

....

....

....

....

....

....

....

BOOK # _____   DATE: _____

Title: _____

Author: _____

Our Book Memories:

....

....

....

....

....

....

....

....

....

....

....

....

....

....

....

....

BOOK # _____   DATE: _____

Title: _____

Author: _____

Our Book Memories:

....

....

....

....

....

....

....

....

....

....

....

....

....

....

....

....

BOOK # _____   DATE: _____

Title: _____

Author: _____

Our Book Memories:

....

....

....

....

....

....

....

....

....

....

....

....

....

....

....

....

....

BOOK # _____   DATE: _____

Title: _____

Author: _____

Our Book Memories:

BOOK # _____   DATE: _____

Title: _____

Author: _____

Our Book Memories:

....

....

....

....

....

....

....

....

....

....

....

....

....

....

....

....

BOOK # _____   DATE: _____

Title: _____

Author: _____

Our Book Memories:

....

....

....

....

....

....

....

....

....

....

....

....

....

....

....

....

BOOK # _____   DATE: _____

Title: _____

Author: _____

Our Book Memories:

BOOK # _____   DATE: _____

Title: _____

Author: _____

Our Book Memories:

....

....

....

....

....

....

....

....

....

....

....

....

....

....

....

....

....

BOOK # _____   DATE: _____

Title: _____

Author: _____

Our Book Memories:

BOOK # _____   DATE: _____

Title: _____

Author: _____

Our Book Memories:

....

....

....

....

....

....

....

....

....

....

....

....

....

....

....

BOOK # _____   DATE: _____

Title: _____

Author: _____

Our Book Memories:

BOOK # _____   DATE: _____

Title: _____

Author: _____

Our Book Memories:

BOOK # _____   DATE: _____

Title: _____

Author: _____

Our Book Memories:

BOOK # _____   DATE: _____

Title: _____

Author: _____

Our Book Memories:

....

....

....

....

....

....

....

....

....

....

....

....

....

....

....

BOOK # _____   DATE: _____

Title: _____

Author: _____

Our Book Memories:

BOOK # _____   DATE: _____

Title: _____

Author: _____

Our Book Memories:

....

....

....

....

....

....

....

....

....

....

....

....

....

....

....

....

BOOK # _____   DATE: _____

Title: _____

Author: _____

Our Book Memories:

BOOK # _____   DATE: _____

Title: _____

Author: _____

Our Book Memories:

....

....

....

....

....

....

....

....

....

....

....

....

....

....

....

....

BOOK # _____   DATE: _____

Title: _____

Author: _____

Our Book Memories:

....

....

....

....

....

....

....

....

....

....

....

....

....

....

....

....

BOOK # _____   DATE: _____

Title: _____

Author: _____

Our Book Memories:

....

....

....

....

....

....

....

....

....

....

....

....

....

....

....

....

BOOK # _____   DATE: _____

Title: _____

Author: _____

Our Book Memories:

....

....

....

....

....

....

....

....

....

....

....

....

....

....

....

BOOK # _____   DATE: _____

Title: _____

Author: _____

Our Book Memories:

....

....

....

....

....

....

....

....

....

....

....

....

....

....

....

....

BOOK # _____   DATE: _____

Title: _____

Author: _____

Our Book Memories:

· ·

· ·

· ·

· ·

· ·

· ·

· ·

· ·

· ·

· ·

· ·

· ·

· ·

· ·

· ·

· ·

BOOK # _____   DATE: _____

Title: _____

Author: _____

Our Book Memories:

....

....

....

....

....

....

....

....

....

....

....

....

....

....

....

....

BOOK # _____   DATE: _____

Title: _____

Author: _____

Our Book Memories:

....

....

....

....

....

....

....

....

....

....

....

....

....

....

....

....

....

BOOK # _____   DATE: _____

Title: _____

Author: _____

Our Book Memories:

....

....

....

....

....

....

....

....

....

....

....

....

....

....

....

....

....

BOOK # _____   DATE: _____

Title: _____

Author: _____

Our Book Memories:

BOOK # _____   DATE: _____

Title: _____

Author: _____

Our Book Memories:

....

....

....

....

....

....

....

....

....

....

....

....

....

....

....

....

....

BOOK # _____   DATE: _____

Title: _____

Author: _____

Our Book Memories:

BOOK # _____   DATE: _____

Title: _____

Author: _____

Our Book Memories:

· ·

· ·

· ·

· ·

· ·

· ·

· ·

· ·

· ·

· ·

· ·

· ·

· ·

· ·

· ·

· ·

BOOK #_____   DATE: _____

Title: _____

Author: _____

Our Book Memories:

....

....

....

....

....

....

....

....

....

....

....

....

....

....

....

....

BOOK # _____   DATE: _____

Title: _____

Author: _____

Our Book Memories:

....

....

....

....

....

....

....

....

....

....

....

....

....

....

....

....

BOOK # _____   DATE: _____

Title: _____

Author: _____

Our Book Memories:

....

....

....

....

....

....

....

....

....

....

....

....

....

....

....

....

BOOK # _____   DATE: _____

Title: _____

Author: _____

Our Book Memories:

....

....

....

....

....

....

....

....

....

....

....

....

....

....

....

BOOK # _____   DATE: _____

Title: _____

Author: _____

Our Book Memories:

....

....

....

....

....

....

....

....

....

....

....

....

....

....

....

....

BOOK # _____   DATE: _____

Title: _____

Author: _____

Our Book Memories:

....

....

....

....

....

....

....

....

....

....

....

....

....

....

....

....

BOOK #_____   DATE: _____

Title: _____

Author: _____

Our Book Memories:

....

....

....

....

....

....

....

....

....

....

....

....

....

....

....

....

BOOK # _____   DATE: _____

Title: _____

Author: _____

Our Book Memories:

....

....

....

....

....

....

....

....

....

....

....

....

....

....

....

BOOK # _____   DATE: _____

Title: _____

Author: _____

Our Book Memories:

BOOK # _____   DATE: _____

Title: _____

Author: _____

Our Book Memories:

BOOK # _____   DATE: _____

Title: _____

Author: _____

Our Book Memories:

....

....

....

....

....

....

....

....

....

....

....

....

....

....

....

....

....

....

BOOK # _____   DATE: _____

Title: _____

Author: _____

Our Book Memories:

....

....

....

....

....

....

....

....

....

....

....

....

....

....

....

....

BOOK # _____   DATE: _____

Title: _____

Author: _____

Our Book Memories:

....

....

....

....

....

....

....

....

....

....

....

....

....

....

....

....

BOOK # _____   DATE: _____

Title: _____

Author: _____

Our Book Memories:

_____

_____

_____

_____

_____

_____

_____

_____

_____

_____

_____

_____

_____

_____

_____

_____

BOOK # _____   DATE: _____

Title: _____

Author: _____

Our Book Memories:

BOOK # _____   DATE: _____

Title: _____

Author: _____

Our Book Memories:

....

....

....

....

....

....

....

....

....

....

....

....

....

....

....

....

BOOK # _____   DATE: _____

Title: _____

Author: _____

Our Book Memories:

....

....

....

....

....

....

....

....

....

....

....

....

....

....

....

....

BOOK # _____   DATE: _____

Title: _____

Author: _____

Our Book Memories:

....

....

....

....

....

....

....

....

....

....

....

....

....

....

....

....

....

BOOK # _____   DATE: _____

Title: _____

Author: _____

Our Book Memories:

....

....

....

....

....

....

....

....

....

....

....

....

....

....

....

....

BOOK # _____   DATE: _____

Title: _____

Author: _____

Our Book Memories:

....

....

....

....

....

....

....

....

....

....

....

....

....

....

....

BOOK # _____   DATE: _____

Title: _____

Author: _____

Our Book Memories:

BOOK # _____   DATE: _____

Title: _____

Author: _____

Our Book Memories:

....

....

....

....

....

....

....

....

....

....

....

....

....

....

....

....

BOOK # _____   DATE: _____

Title: _____

Author: _____

Our Book Memories:

....

....

....

....

....

....

....

....

....

....

....

....

....

....

....

....

BOOK # _____   DATE: _____

Title: _____

Author: _____

Our Book Memories:

....

....

....

....

....

....

....

....

....

....

....

....

....

....

....

....

BOOK # _____   DATE: _____

Title: _____

Author: _____

Our Book Memories:

BOOK # _____   DATE: _____

Title: _____

Author: _____

Our Book Memories:

....

....

....

....

....

....

....

....

....

....

....

....

....

....

....

....

BOOK # _____   DATE: _____

Title: _____

Author: _____

Our Book Memories:

BOOK # _____   DATE: _____

Title: _____

Author: _____

Our Book Memories:

....

....

....

....

....

....

....

....

....

....

....

....

....

....

....

....

BOOK # _____   DATE: _____

Title: _____

Author: _____

Our Book Memories:

BOOK # _____   DATE: _____

Title: _____

Author: _____

Our Book Memories:

....

....

....

....

....

....

....

....

....

....

....

....

....

....

....

....

....

BOOK # _____   DATE: _____

Title: _____

Author: _____

Our Book Memories:

....

....

....

....

....

....

....

....

....

....

....

....

....

....

....

....

BOOK # _____   DATE: _____

Title: _____

Author: _____

Our Book Memories:

BOOK # _____   DATE: _____

Title: _____

Author: _____

Our Book Memories:

BOOK # _____   DATE: _____

Title: _____

Author: _____

Our Book Memories:

....

....

....

....

....

....

....

....

....

....

....

....

....

....

....

....

BOOK # _____   DATE: _____

Title: _____

Author: _____

Our Book Memories:

....

....

....

....

....

....

....

....

....

....

....

....

....

....

....

....

BOOK # _____   DATE: _____

Title: _____

Author: _____

Our Book Memories:

BOOK # _____   DATE: _____

Title: _____

Author: _____

Our Book Memories:

....

....

....

....

....

....

....

....

....

....

....

....

....

....

....

....

....

BOOK # _____   DATE: _____

Title: _____

Author: _____

Our Book Memories:

BOOK # _____   DATE: _____

Title: _____

Author: _____

Our Book Memories:

....

....

....

....

....

....

....

....

....

....

....

....

....

....

....

....

BOOK # _____   DATE: _____

Title: _____

Author: _____

Our Book Memories:

....

....

....

....

....

....

....

....

....

....

....

....

....

....

....

....

BOOK # _____ DATE: _____

Title: _____

Author: _____

Our Book Memories:

BOOK # _____   DATE: _____

Title: _____

Author: _____

Our Book Memories:

....

....

....

....

....

....

....

....

....

....

....

....

....

....

....

....

....

BOOK # _____   DATE: _____

Title: _____

Author: _____

Our Book Memories:

BOOK # _____   DATE: _____

Title: _____

Author: _____

Our Book Memories:

BOOK # _____   DATE: _____

Title: _____

Author: _____

Our Book Memories:

....

....

....

....

....

....

....

....

....

....

....

....

....

....

....

....

BOOK # _____   DATE: _____

Title: _____

Author: _____

Our Book Memories:

BOOK # _____   DATE: _____

Title: _____

Author: _____

Our Book Memories:

BOOK # _____ DATE: _____

Title: _____

Author: _____

Our Book Memories:

BOOK # _____   DATE: _____

Title: _____

Author: _____

Our Book Memories:

BOOK # _____   DATE: _____

Title: _____

Author: _____

Our Book Memories:

BOOK # _____   DATE: _____

Title: _____

Author: _____

Our Book Memories:

BOOK # _____   DATE: _____

Title: _____

Author: _____

Our Book Memories:

....

....

....

....

....

....

....

....

....

....

....

....

....

....

....

....

....

BOOK # _____   DATE: _____

Title: _____

Author: _____

Our Book Memories:

....

....

....

....

....

....

....

....

....

....

....

....

....

....

....

....

BOOK # _____   DATE: _____

Title: _____

Author: _____

Our Book Memories:

....

....

....

....

....

....

....

....

....

....

....

....

....

....

....

....

....

....

BOOK # _____   DATE: _____

Title: _____

Author: _____

Our Book Memories:

....

....

....

....

....

....

....

....

....

....

....

....

....

....

....

....

....

BOOK # _____   DATE: _____

Title: _____

Author: _____

Our Book Memories:

....

....

....

....

....

....

....

....

....

....

....

....

....

....

....

....

....

BOOK # _____   DATE: _____

Title: _____

Author: _____

Our Book Memories:

....

....

....

....

....

....

....

....

....

....

....

....

....

....

....

....

BOOK # _____   DATE: _____

Title: _____

Author: _____

Our Book Memories:

....

....

....

....

....

....

....

....

....

....

....

....

....

....

....

....

BOOK # _____   DATE: _____

Title: _____

Author: _____

Our Book Memories:

BOOK # _____   DATE: _____

Title: _____

Author: _____

Our Book Memories:

··

··

··

··

··

··

··

··

··

··

··

··

··

··

··

··

BOOK # _____   DATE: _____

Title: _____

Author: _____

Our Book Memories:

....

....

....

....

....

....

....

....

....

....

....

....

....

....

....

....

BOOK # _____   DATE: _____

Title: _____

Author: _____

Our Book Memories:

....

....

....

....

....

....

....

....

....

....

....

....

....

....

....

....

....

BOOK # _____   DATE: _____

Title: _____

Author: _____

Our Book Memories:

BOOK # _____   DATE: _____

Title: _____

Author: _____

Our Book Memories:

....

....

....

....

....

....

....

....

....

....

....

....

....

....

....

....

BOOK # _____   DATE: _____

Title: _____

Author: _____

Our Book Memories:

....

....

....

....

....

....

....

....

....

....

....

....

....

....

....

....

BOOK # _____   DATE: _____

Title: _____

Author: _____

Our Book Memories:

....

....

....

....

....

....

....

....

....

....

....

....

....

....

....

....

BOOK # _____ !   DATE: _____

Title: _____

Author: _____

Our Book Memories:

··

··

··

··

··

··

··

··

··

··

··

··

··

··

··

··

We Did It!

the _____ Family

Completed the

100 Book Read-Aloud

Family Challenge!

Congratulations!

Made in the USA
Monee, IL
17 September 2020